Karma is not always a b*tch

Karma McKay

BookLeaf
Publishing

Presentation by *BookLeaf Publishing*

Web: www.bookleafpub.com

E-mail: info@bookleafpub.com

ISBN: 978-93-95890-52-6

First edition 2022

DEDICATION

To all my cheerleaders who have not given up. Annalisa, Mom, and Aura and Mrs. DeShane.

PREFACE

Karma is a poet of the many life experiences she has endured. She aims to be a voice of those that have none. Advocating and helping is her favourite thing to do.

September 7th

First day of many, this opportunity came at just the right time.

As the early days of this book, I have been decaying in a mental health hospital grasping at something- anything to live for.

Good morning sun, I feel your beams in my chest; in my soul and mouth. You have given me the ability to write and astound, and with that, I begin my book.

Diving in

I see daises and feel like one of them, flowing in the wind with my other queer folks. Laughing, crying, and most of all, growing. As a former addict and trauma survivor, I see things differently. Seeing myself engulfed in sewage, when all I wanted is a warm shower. When I saw myself in mainly the sewer when rats were friends. Even though no longer, it was my life for years. Yet, here I am, eating bananas and fresh blackberries. Admiring the warmth of the berries on my tongue. This is after I opened up the circular grate and flew out like an imprisoned dove, then screaming at the top of my lungs, "I, am, free!"

Mother Nature

It's like I'm looking through a crystal ball;
etching every thought into it with my acrylic
nails, only, I'm looking at the past. It's lonely
there. It's scary there. Carve my tone of tune into
this melancholy dreary brokenness. I open my
new gel eye relaxer with the same nails as I just
mentioned. Knowing my eyes are burnt like two
piss holes in the snow, mother please don't die
our eyes can relax now we don't have to peer
into hidden meanings like an iridescent Rubik's
cube. I miss her and the only thing I know about
her after this past year of sobriety is that she's
still struggling, please cast a spell on me and
make it so I can't carry care in my cornea this
long lasting day you live over and over again. I
think you need glasses, or maybe contact lenses?
I don't wonder which one any more. Eating the
fields of wheat and corn with the perplexed gaze
of the optic nerve as far I as it can see. You're
missing your mom I'm missing you we are
missing drugs and booze. Goodnight.

Change is a monster

I feel the whirlwind of change.

Clawing my way up to the very esophagus that swallowed me, took a bite of my being with its plaqued teeth, chewed me up, spit me out when I wasn't sweet enough for the buds of the dirty growing flowers that are on his tongue.

His stomach and saliva can't be the antidote for my copper attitude.
Dying, I was. Dying, I will be. Dying, I was never.

But.. laugh I could.

Uncomfortable feelings in the styrofoam pit that the kids fall into to learn they can trust something other than the arms of the caregiver.

I will…. Over… come…
this….that…..breaks…me.

 Earthling, open your arms, I…am …home.

Suburban Paradise

Nights like this make me happy to be inside; and dare I say it; but alive. As the mixture of snow-like-rain crunches under my fur slippers I can feel the luck melt every snowflake that hits my body, almost as if the glee of my unhomelessness brings a kind of warmth to the outside of my carcass where the ogre of melancholy once took home in my frail arachnoid cyst. The twist in my bowel he made with his giant green and warted hands. But, today he is not here any more. This body is now a soup of carrots and grass fed beef, roasted in the suburbs; I'm almost describing my dream home. THATS THE POINT THIS BODY IS A DREAM HOME NEVER CAN ANYONE ELSE RIP DOWN THESE DOORS IM IN MY SUBURBAN PARADISE

"Mermaids need air too"

And as you foreshadowed in my past, here I am, crossing my equator for the first time. The pirates of the Somalian sea are far past gone and the whales are moving with me as I walk down the steepest stairs of my sail ship and shave my head for the tattoo I saw whilst I was underwater, gasping for air, there she was, oh sweet mermaid of the ocean deep deep on the coral reef, moving her hair with my telepathic orca orchestra. "Grow" she said "grow like the islands I sun bathe on, and don't forget, we all need air sometimes too"

Drugs are like wolves

Good morning rays of sunshine, I love you but I also loved drugs. oh dear god why did you plant addiction into my sweet brain that could have gone without it. I love flowers I love earrings I loved drugs- wait; no more drugs. This is all me now. Torn to shreds by a forklift tire that ran over the tiniest part of what I had left of my dignity. Eaten by the wolves of addiction. BUT regurgitated and painted back together with gold and silver lining
I AM ALIVE DEAR ANIMALS FEAR THIS NEW ME
Foolish animals, don't even know what it's like to be reborn.

Stand with Ukraine

Enough about me, this world needs attention. I
cannot begin to fathom the Ukrainian people in
this rubble of their used-to-be habitat. They
would sing, dance, write, learn, and just be.

Now, they are hiding.
Opening their creaky water-stained basements to
their cousins of humanity.

Complete strangers become home and these
people just want their babies and daughters and
aunts and dads back.

I can't do much about that. But I can walk with
them in my cob-webbed dreams.

Please know, I am here.

Cubs turn into lions real quick

Cooped up, I cried. Cooped up, I sang myself to sleep.
I don't know what "cooped up" means yet but it's somewhere along the lines of a bird learning to sing again, in the very cage it lost it's voice.
Or a lion roaring after a long battle with man.
Alone, desperate for love, for something other than cruelty on one self.
 It bit down into its own fur, into its own flesh long ago but, now, with a limp, It will run free once more, if only for once more.
But it knows it'll be thousands more.
Once it's not comparable to desreetness of the tamed soul of the new found lion.

I AM LION WILD AND FREE. HEAR ROARS AND WATCH ME FROLIC IN MASSIVE BODIES OF WHEAT AND SOIL, ONLY TO PICK UP A CAMERA AND SAY WOW, SHES FINALLY FREE

Saying goodbye to the shelter

Showers run 24/7. Is this an act of kindness or
something to wash the tears of our forgotten
sisters yes I'm talking about the indigenous
women lost;

I don't mean that sister you lost over a turkey
dinner: please hear me; dear shelter do you
know what it's like to be wanted??

I'll cry till my heart runs out of feeling and the
meth pipe drowns my mouth out with smoke.

Why don't you care? You care more about my
sobriety while I stay here clubbed feet curled up
in a blanket with who??

You.

You.

You.

Open my mind up why do you want to hear it till
you don't?

Shame, shame, shame on you.

This is all dead shelter this is it.

Goodbye.

"Hey, how are you?"

Can't be bothered for small talk. Hey how are
the kids? Is your husband still grasping at straws
to get you to open your legs one more time for
that "perfect" child? See? I can't even do it right.
Good morning does your mom know you're
wearing that? I try to say the "hey how are ya"s
but I'm terribly brought closer to awkward
inappropriate comments and I cry into my older
sisters Instagram. This is not what I am used to.
I eat the comments like burnt toast I know I need
to but I don't particularly want to. And again,
that's it, that's all. Broken dreams and all I open
my mouth skittishly remembering I have no
place for small talk. Let that ruminate.

Is this what trauma taste like?

Sore knuckles from keeping a fist formation for so long turned into the melody of pain which sounded so difficult it was almost comfortable. Now, the branches swinging into the abyss of air by wind pouring its own push and pull scenario into this body of plant is a new song of soul. Melody of not-so-stillness. I am new and I know I say this often but it is always true, actually not always, but more so time after time I type this with my shaking thumbs. A growing crop forms its own group of acapello singers but also one artist, the artist of Mother Nature. Beautiful, she is. Eating my bacteria brain true hallucinations like growing tadpoles on dead skin on an ankle under water. This is what life is meant for. This is what we are meant for. I am alive here, and fuck I'm proud to have name, body and soul of hope. Three cheers to sobriety and gratitude.

Recovery is worth everything

I don't mean to be a disturbance but I am disturbed; I'm clean but also facing hell; like a dog barking at the moon, I am envious of its light and beauty. Do I belong on this earth? I will never figure it out until I prove I do. Life is funny like that; beauty is more than curled hair and lipstick. Beauty is sweat collecting on the ripples of my forehead when I'm running from the voice in my ears. Or brain? They say it's my mind playing tricks but it seems like I'm only useful for talking to them about the pain they put me through over, over, over again. Barking at the lighting of the moon is exactly what I would like to do. Telling them I'm worth the light and life. I am not trying to be beautiful. Trauma isn't beautiful. But recovery is. Getting better is worth barking at the moon for. I will greet the moon every night with my bleached tips and silver blue splotches in my roots. This, this is beauty.

Please, father, let me forget you.

Opening your hands to catch something sweet from a friend, this is sharing. But sharing does not mean I must take my skirt off my legs after being concussed in my frontal lobe to be wanted. Sharing includes far more than material. It includes empathy, a good laugh, and most of all, stories. I was only old enough to grasp at this idea about a decade ago. This is when I had no material and felt purposeless until harmonizing my brain and lungs in an open casket, telling my father he will never be forgotten. Yet, we are forgetting. And that is why I am proud.

Shame is maladaptive

Sometimes, I get so angry, I start to cry. I sob and can't help but think of things that make me more angry and cry some more. Do you ever get that? An avalanche of anger. A storm of rage. A hurricane of fear. Oops did I say fear? What I meant was discomfort. But isn't that the same thing? I suppose my "typo" was just a hypothesis of realness. A synopsis of my pain. When I am angry, I'm usually riddled with fear. But I usually can't comprehend this. I'm usually too pissed off to bring the grief of depicting what emotion my anger is stemming from. But then again, who would I be if I wasn't angry, disgusted, or ashamed? It's all I know. I used to live and breathe shame. But now I am much more than that. I am the bringer of gratitude, the bargainer with my unsettling thoughts, I am starting to realize; I am much more than shame.

We are all guinea pigs

Sunday quenches Saturday's mouth and tongue like a honey crisp apple on a guinea pigs mouth who hasn't been fed in weeks. Basking itself in the beauty of what it's like to be nourished again. Except, I am the guinea pig on a Sunday- wait there are too many metaphors to explain what it is I'm trying to say. I AM THE GUINEA PIG. So please, feed me your apple peels. Allow me to grow from your scraps. AND DO NOT FORGET I AM ALIVE TOO.

Purposeful life

Have you ever mistaken a pharmacy for an opportunity? Or a ocean for your eternal haven? Have you ever been broken? Yes, broken crayons still colour the same but don't the less diminished ones get picked first? How old were you when you realized that? A man asks for food from me after I tried to take my own life. I gave him what I used to wash down the pills. He was so grateful he gave me props not knowing what I had just done. Then, in that moment, I knew I was not disposable. I was meant to be in that moment at that time to help that man. And I am meant to be alive right now. Diminished, yes, but all I need is a crayon sharpener.

Amnesia

Velcro and belts hold down my arms and legs to a bed I did not ask to be in- I am dizzy- I start to shed tears thinking of how it all started. I was about 13 when I first took too many drugs. But instead of calling 911 I just sat there, heart racing, hallucinating, seeing men walk around my room. Then, I tried to sleep for I had school the next day. But I felt numb and I liked that. Cutting is another story I am not ready to mention at this point-yesterday- I woke up in an mri machine at some hospital in Toronto-my cat came to me in my dream and said it will be over soon. But I don't know what he meant.

Positive thoughts are hard to come by

It's been a while since I felt this level of hope. And it looks good on me. The darkness was long and painful but now I see the pink and orange translucent orbs of the sun beginning to shine. The sun is funny like that, it often goes away and the darkness is cold and scary. As the sun wakes up I can almost taste my hopes and dreams. And as I should. I have been through too much to not be seeing the positives come to life. A silver lining in the depths of my worst days. Today is another good day despite some not so positive things. I do not need to let my symptoms define me. I am grateful for my resilience and ability to function. And I accept the struggle of finding myself after a long time of being lost in an abyss of monsters and flashbacks. When it is all said and done I will bring myself to this moment and celebrate how far I have come. But one breath leads to another and one day at a time leads to my goals being achieved. I am grateful for life in this moment.

Goodbye

Here we are, at the end of the book. I hope after reading this you know your worth is far from nothing. My lashes quiver with twitches when the sun is too bright, but you are the sun. Some eyes just can't handle it. You can shine so bright. I love you.